ISAAC ASIMOV'S
Library of the Universe

The
Space
Spotter's
Guide

ST. GABRIEL SCHOOL

by Isaac Asimov

520
ASI

Gareth Stevens Publishing
Milwaukee

A special thanks to Julian Baum and Richard Baum.

The reproduction rights to all photographs and
illustrations in this book are controlled by the
individuals or institutions credited on page 32 and
may not be reproduced without their permission.

Library of Congress Cataloging-in-Publication Data

Asimov, Isaac, 1920-
    Space spotter's guide.

    (Isaac Asimov's library of the universe)
    Bibliography: p.
    Includes index.
    Summary: Provides tips on how to spot some of the wonders of our solar
system and galaxy and how to choose a telescope. Also discusses
astronomical mysteries and amazing facts.
    1. Astronomy--Juvenile literature. 2. Astronomy--Observers' manuals--
Juvenile literature. [1. Astronomy--Observers' manuals] I. Title. II. Series:
Asimov, Isaac, 1920-   . Library of the universe.
QB46.A79   1988   520   87-42600
ISBN 1-55532-356-1 (lib. bdg.)
ISBN 1-55532-381-2

A Gareth Stevens Children's Books edition

Edited, designed, and produced by
Gareth Stevens, Inc.   7317 West Green Tree Road   Milwaukee, Wisconsin 53223, USA

Text copyright © 1989 by Nightfall, Inc.
End matter copyright © 1989 by Gareth Stevens, Inc. and Martin Greenberg
Format copyright © 1989 by Gareth Stevens, Inc.

First published in the United States and Canada in 1989 by Gareth Stevens, Inc.
All rights reserved. No part of this book may be reproduced or utilized in any form or by
any means without permission in writing from Gareth Stevens, Inc.

Cover photograph © Frank Zullo 1988
Designer: Laurie Shock
Picture research: Kathy Keller
Artwork commissioning: Kathy Keller and Laurie Shock
Project editor: Mark Sachner
Research editor: Scott Enk
Technical advisers and consulting editors: Greg Walz-Chojnacki and Francis Reddy

2 3 4 5 6 7 8 9 94 93 92 91 90 89

CONTENTS

Our Changing Sky 4
Earth's Neighbor 6
Stars for All Seasons 8
The Stars of Spring 10
The Stars of Summer 12
The Stars of Autumn 14
The Stars of Winter 16
Sky Wanderers 18
Venus and Mercury 20
The Outer Planets 22
Choosing a Telescope 24
Viewing Deep Space 26

Fact File 28
More Books About Astronomy 30
Places to Visit 30
For More Information About Astronomy 30
Glossary 31
Index 32

Nowadays, we have seen planets up close, all the way to distant Uranus. We have seen dead volcanoes on Mars and live ones on Io, one of Jupiter's moons. We have detected strange objects no one knew anything about until recently: quasars, pulsars, black holes. We have learned amazing facts about how the Universe was born, and have some ideas about how it might die. Nothing could be more astonishing and more interesting.

Of course, few of us will ever be able to go out into space. And few of us even have the advanced instruments needed to make interesting new discoveries about the Universe. But we can all look at the stars with the help of binoculars or small telescopes in places away from the bright lights and dust of a big city.

In this book, you will learn how to spot some of the wonders of our Solar system, our Galaxy, and beyond!

Isaac Asimov

Our Changing Sky

The sky changes as we watch! Through the night, we see stars rise and set, turning in large circles about a spot in the sky near Polaris. That's because Earth is turning on its axis.

Polaris is also called the North Star, because it is almost directly above Earth's North Pole. Because of this, it doesn't move, but always stays in the north.

From night to night, the sky shifts, too. A pattern of stars at midnight on one night won't return exactly until a whole year has passed. So the patterns change with the seasons. That's because Earth revolves around the Sun.

Left: The Sun, Moon, and stars appear to wheel across the sky, an illusion caused by the spinning planet on which we live.

Earth's Neighbor

As you might guess, the brightest object in the night sky is the Moon. The Moon shines by reflected light from the Sun. When the Moon and Sun are on opposite sides of Earth, we see the Moon's lighted side as a "full Moon" shining all night.

When the Moon and Sun are on the same side of the Earth, we face the Moon's unlighted side. Perhaps we see just a bit of the lighted side as a crescent just after sunset. From night to night, the crescent gets thicker until there is a full Moon, and then thinner and thinner until there is a "new Moon."

The Moon goes around the Earth in a little less than a month. In that time, we see all its shapes, or phases, in order.

Stonehenge — a prehistoric observatory?

Before modern astronomical instruments were invented, people had their own ways of watching the stars. In England, there is a circle of large upright stones with other stones in the center. It is called Stonehenge. Some astronomers think Stonehenge might be what is left of a prehistoric observatory! Did ancient astronomers look across the stones to see where the Sun would rise at the summer solstice — or to predict Lunar eclipses? We can't be sure.

The phases of the Moon. The Moon's appearance changes as it orbits
Earth each month.

A dramatic shot of our nearest neighbor in space.

BIG DIPPER

Polaris

Dubhe

Merak

CASSIOPEIA

WEST   NORTH   EAST

Stars for All Seasons

From the Northern Hemisphere, we see certain patterns of
stars, or constellations, circling Polaris. They never set and
are always visible. There are some stars that circle a point
above the South Pole, opposite Polaris. A constellation
called the Southern Cross, or Crux, points to the place the
southern stars circle about. But in the Northern Hemisphere,
we never see this part of the sky!

The chief northern constellation is Ursa Major, the Great Bear. This constellation includes the seven stars of the Big Dipper. The two stars at the bowl end of the dipper are called the "pointers." Follow an imaginary line through them to find Polaris. On the other side of Polaris from the Big Dipper are five stars in a "W" shape. This constellation is Cassiopeia (pronounced cass-ee-o-PEEH-uh), the Queen.

Left: The Big Dipper and Cassiopeia are visible all year round in the northern hemisphere.

Below: If you looked in the northern sky at the same time each night, you'd see the Big Dipper and Cassiopeia slowly chase each other around Polaris, the North Star.

WINTER　　　　　　　SPRING

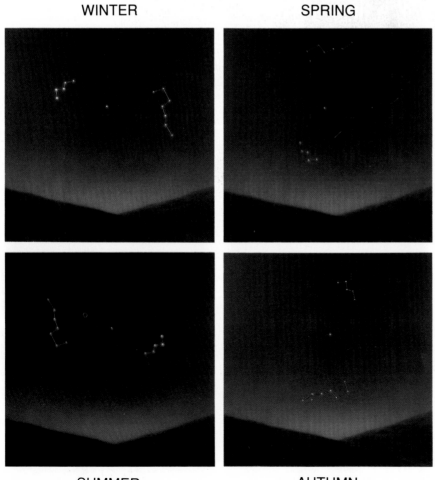

SUMMER　　　　　　　AUTUMN

The Stars of Spring

For the next eight pages, each sky picture points you toward the south. As you face south, imagine that the top of the picture is folded toward you and passes over your head. The bottom of the picture would then be south, and the top would be north.

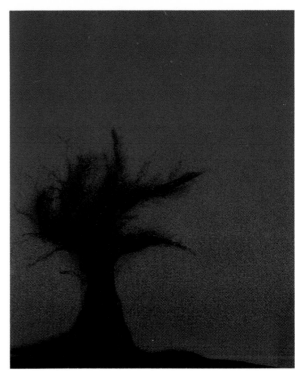

As you face south in the spring and look way up over your head, the Big Dipper will stretch across the sky above you. If you follow the curve of the handle of the Big Dipper back toward the southern part of the sky, you will come upon the constellation Boötes (pronounced bo-OH-taze), the Herdsman. One part of Boötes is Arcturus (ark-TOOR-us), which is one of the brightest stars in the spring sky.

Continue to follow the imaginary curve south, and you will come to the constellation Virgo, the Maiden, and its bright star, Spica (SPEE-kuh). To the west (right as you face south) of Virgo is the constellation Leo, the Lion, with its bright star, Regulus.

Virgo and Leo are two of the 12 constellations of the zodiac (ZO-dee-ak). The Sun, Moon, and planets travel through the zodiac as they move across the sky.

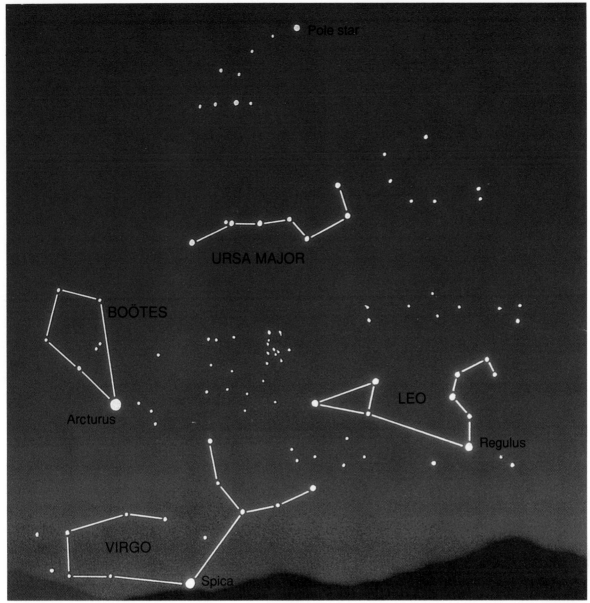

Pole star

URSA MAJOR

BOÖTES

Arcturus

LEO

Regulus

VIRGO

Spica

EAST   SOUTH   WEST

Above: With the Big Dipper overhead, look for Boötes and the bright star Arcturus in the east, Virgo in the south, and Leo in the west.

Right: the Zodiac of Dendera — a star map of ancient Egypt.

The Stars of Summer

One of the easiest constellations to spot in the summer sky is Sagittarius (saj-it-TAIR-ee-us), the Archer. Its outline looks like a teapot in the southern sky.

The Milky Way, a band of foggy light that encircles the sky, passes through Sagittarius and is brightest there. If you use a small telescope, you can see many stars in the Milky Way.

To the west, right of Sagittarius as you face south, is a curve of stars. This constellation is Scorpius (SCORE-peeh-us), the Scorpion, with its bright red star, Antares (an-TAR-eze). Antares is a "red giant," hundreds of times wider than our Sun.

Over your head as you face south, and halfway between Sagittarius and Polaris, is Lyra (LIE-ruh), the Lyre, with its bright star, Vega (VAY-guh). To the east of Lyra is Cygnus (SIG-nus), the Swan, with its bright star, Deneb (DEN-eb). Halfway between Deneb and Sagittarius is the bright star Altair, in Aquila (ACK-wuh-luh), the Eagle. The three stars Vega, Deneb, and Altair form a star pattern we call the "Summer Triangle."

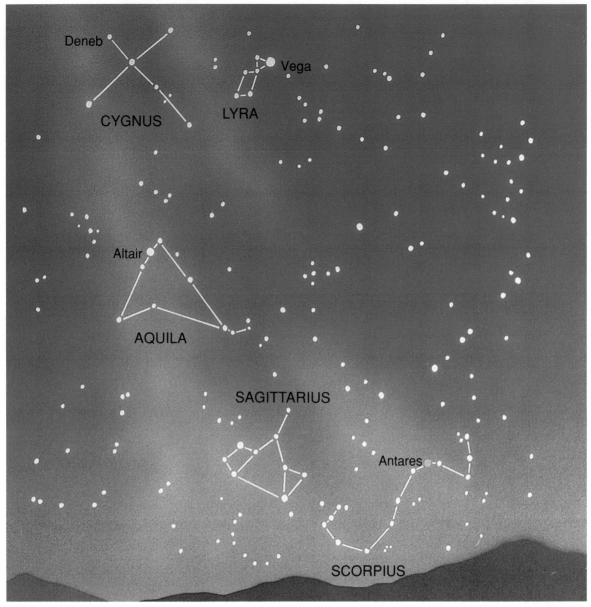

Deneb

Vega

CYGNUS

LYRA

Altair

AQUILA

SAGITTARIUS

Antares

SCORPIUS

EAST   SOUTH   WEST

Above: Lyra shines overhead, with Cygnus off to
the east and Aquila to the south. Farther south and
west lie Sagittarius and Scorpius.

Right: Sagittarius, the Archer.

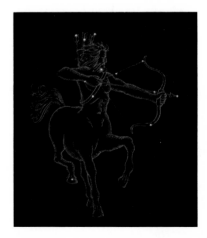

The Stars of Autumn

The constellation Pegasus, the Flying Horse, is high up in the autumn sky (nearly overhead as you face south). Its four bright stars form the Square of Pegasus. Immediately to its northeast (above and to the left of Pegasus), is Andromeda (an-DROM-uh-duh), the Chained Maiden. Andromeda is exciting because within it, you can just barely spot a small, foggy patch of light.

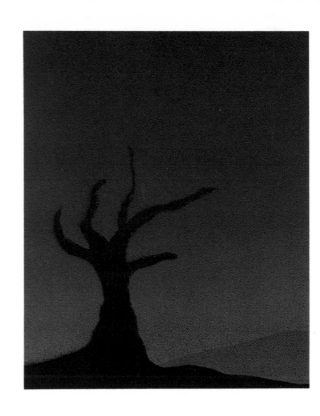

If we look at this patch through a telescope, it turns out to be a huge collection of stars called the Andromeda Galaxy.

To the southeast of Pegasus (lower left as you face south) is Cetus (SEE-tus), the Whale, which has a rather dim star that is variable. A variable star grows brighter, then dimmer. When astronomers first saw this star, this changing brightness seemed so unusual that they named the star Mira (MEER-uh), which means "wonderful."

How far away can we see?

The most distant object we can clearly see without a telescope is the Andromeda Galaxy. It looks like a dim, fuzzy star, but it is really a galaxy larger than our own. It is about 2.3 million light-years away. But we can see still farther <u>with</u> a telescope. For instance, the nearest quasar is about a billion light-years away, and others might be as many as 17 billion light-years away. Astronomers don't expect to see many things much farther away than that!

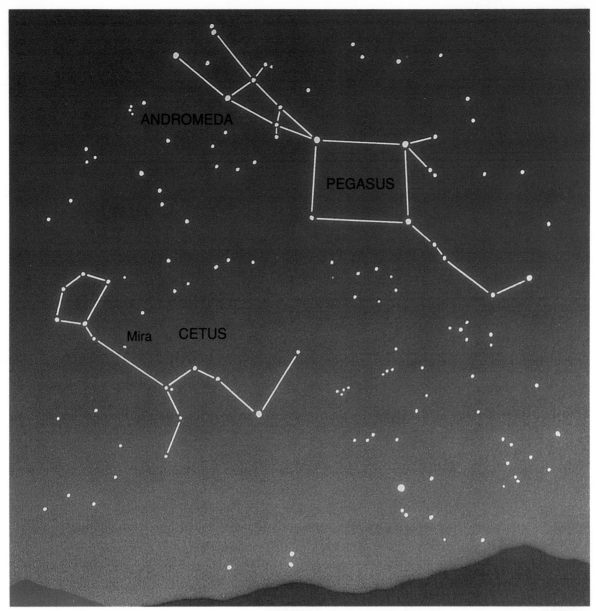

EAST   SOUTH   WEST

Above: Three large
constellations dominate the
autumn sky — Pegasus,
Andromeda, and Cetus.

Right: Andromeda contains
the farthest object visible to
the unaided eye — galaxy
M31, the Andromeda Galaxy.
Its light has traveled for over
two million years before
reaching us!

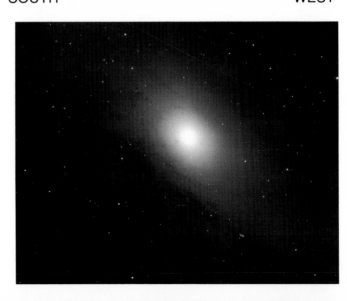

15

The Stars of Winter

In the cold winter sky, you can see Orion (oh-RI-un), the Hunter. This beautiful constellation can help you find other star groups in the winter sky. On Orion's northeastern edge (the upper left, as you face south) is the huge red giant star called Betelgeuse (BEE-tul-jooz). Orion's southwestern edge (lower right) is marked by Rigel (RI-jel), a star about 55,000 times brighter than our Sun.

Between these two bright stars is a row of three stars, Orion's belt. Below the belt is another row of stars, Orion's sword. The middle "star" of the sword is actually a huge cloud of gas and dust called the Orion Nebula. Orion's belt points down and to the left (southeast) at the bright star Sirius (SIR-ee-us), in Canis Major, the Great Dog. Sirius is the brightest star visible from Earth — not counting the Sun, of course!

The belt also points up and to the right (northwest) toward Aldebaran (al-DEB-air-en), the brightest star in Taurus, the Bull.

Did Sirius change color?

Some ancient writers describe Sirius as red. But we can see that Sirius is a brilliant <u>white</u> star. Could it have been red in ancient times and have turned white? Astronomers don't see how. Of course, the ancient Egyptians watched Sirius rise with the Sun so they would know when the Nile River would flood. When it rose, Sirius might have looked reddish, just as the Sun does. That might have started people thinking of Sirius as red. But we can't be sure!

TAURUS   PLEIADES

Aldebaran

Betelgeuse   ORION

Procyon

Rigel

Sirius

CANIS MAJOR

EAST   SOUTH   WEST

Above: Sirius, the brightest
star in the sky, gleams in the
southeast. Orion and Taurus,
nearly due south, shine
higher up.

Right: With binoculars, you
may notice that the middle
star of the three hanging off
Orion's belt looks fuzzy and
greenish. It's really the Orion
Nebula, a giant gas cloud in
which stars are born.

Sky Wanderers

Not all the objects in the sky turn in one group or follow the same path.

The Moon moves across the sky through the 12 constellations of the zodiac, making its complete circle in a little less than a month. The Sun moves along the same path. But it moves much more slowly, staying in each constellation of the zodiac for one month and making its complete circuit in a year.

Five bright, starlike objects — Mercury, Venus, Mars, Jupiter, and Saturn — also move along the zodiac. These also take different lengths of time to move across the sky. For example, Jupiter takes almost 12 years to circle the sky, while Saturn takes more than 29.

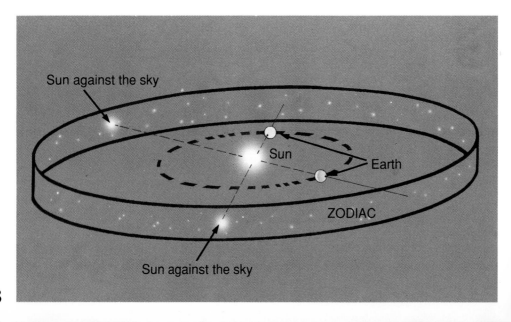

Sun against the sky

Sun

Earth

ZODIAC

Sun against the sky

Above: the zodiac constellations. Clockwise from the top: Leo, Cancer, Gemini, Taurus, Aries, Pisces, Aquarius, Capricorn, Sagittarius, Scorpius, Libra, and Virgo.

Left: As Earth moves in its yearly orbit around the Sun, it is the Sun that appears to move against the background of stars in the sky. The constellations it moves through make up the zodiac.

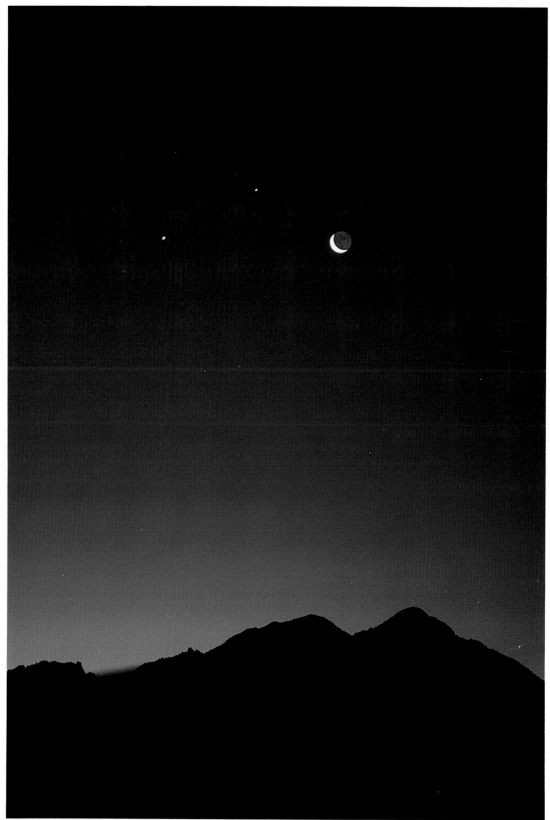

A naked-eye view of brilliant Venus and dim Mercury as they line up
with a crescent Moon.

Venus and Mercury

Venus and Mercury are closer to the Sun than we are. For that reason, we always see them near the Sun. Naturally, we can't see them in the daytime.

But when the Sun sets, Venus is sometimes in the western sky as the brilliant Evening Star, setting a couple of hours later. When it is on the other side of the Sun, it shines in the eastern sky before dawn as the Morning Star.

Mercury is even closer to the Sun, but it is dimmer, so it is harder to observe. But through a telescope, you can see that both Mercury and Venus show phases, just as the Moon does.

Two satellite photos. Above: The clouds of Venus reflect sunlight, making the planet appear very bright. Below: Mercury, with its barren, cratered surface, is much harder to see.

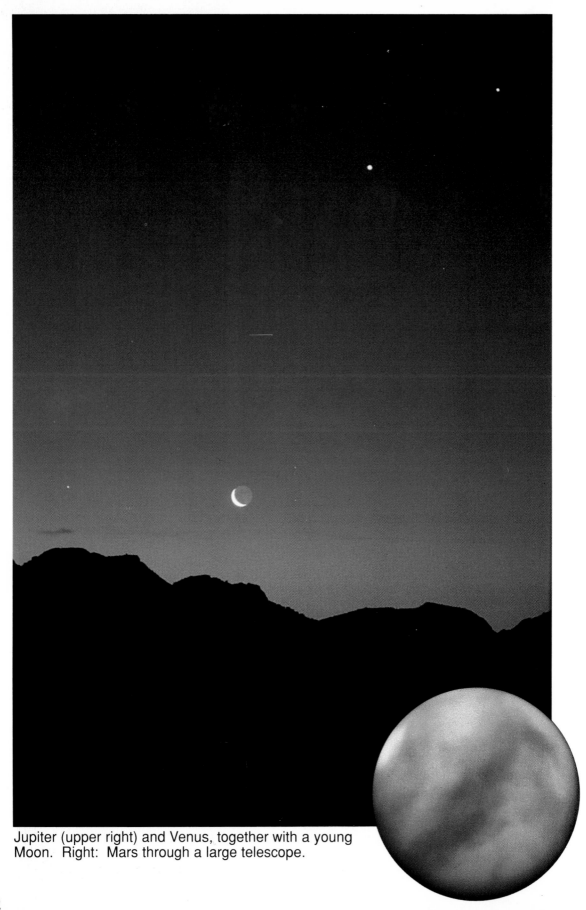

Jupiter (upper right) and Venus, together with a young
Moon. Right: Mars through a large telescope.

The Outer Planets

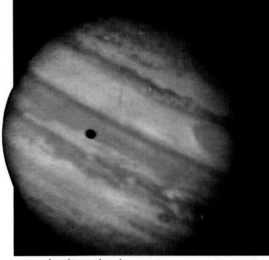

Jupiter, the largest known planet.

Mars, Jupiter, and Saturn are all farther from the Sun than Earth is. They can all shine in the midnight sky. Since we always see their sunlit portions, they are always "full" when we see them.

Mars is reddish in color. Jupiter and Saturn are giant planets. Through the telescope, you can see Jupiter as a small globe, along with its four large satellites. Saturn has a bright ring of ice and rock particles circling it, and it is one of the most beautiful sights in the heavens.

There are still farther planets: Uranus, Neptune, and Pluto. You can see Uranus and Neptune easily with a small telescope, but you need a large one to see Pluto.

Saturn, the ringed beauty.

How far is "far" in space?

The farthest known planet in our Solar system is Pluto. Traveling at 186,000 miles (300,000 km) a second, light takes about 5 1/2 hours to reach us from Pluto. The nearest star, Alpha Centauri, is so far away that its light takes 4.3 years to reach us. We say it is 4.3 light-years away. Other stars, of course, are much farther, and our Milky Way Galaxy, a huge collection of stars shaped like a pinwheel, is about 100,000 light-years from end to end!

Choosing a Telescope

For some purposes, a good pair of binoculars is fine for viewing the heavens. You can watch for artificial satellites, study the surface of the Moon, and see comets in greater detail. But you can do all this and more with a telescope!

Telescopes come in two varieties: refracting and reflecting. Refractors use lenses to concentrate the light. Reflectors use curved mirrors to concentrate the light.

You might want to use a machine called a drive mechanism to keep your telescope turning with the sky. Or you might want filters to watch eclipses and special cameras for taking photographs. It takes money and experience to use these things, so it is best to start as simply as possible if you decide to get a telescope.

In a refracting telescope, a large lens collects and focuses light to the eyepiece.

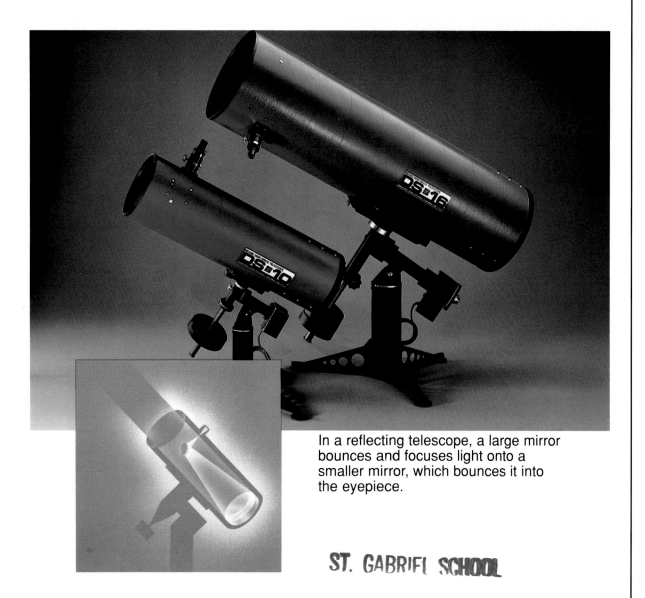

In a reflecting telescope, a large mirror bounces and focuses light onto a smaller mirror, which bounces it into the eyepiece.

ST. GABRIEL SCHOOL

The tiniest stars pack a powerful punch!

Stars like Betelgeuse are hundreds of times wider than the Sun. Others are pushed together so tightly that they are smaller than our Earth, but contain as much matter as the Sun. One type is white-hot, so it is called a white dwarf. But even tighter, smaller stars are possible. If all the particles in our Sun were pushed together until they touched, the Sun would be only eight miles (13 km) across! Stars like this, called neutron stars, actually exist.

Viewing Deep Space

The stars we see with our eyes alone are almost all quite near us. With telescopes, we can see objects farther off.

There are star clusters, each of which might contain thousands of stars. The largest star cluster is in the constellation of Hercules.

You can also use a telescope to see distant galaxies that lie far beyond our Milky Way. Each contains hundreds of billions of stars! The Andromeda Galaxy is one of the closest. Some of these galaxies look like oval bits of fog. Some look like pinwheels and are called spiral galaxies.

From Earth, the spiral Whirlpool Galaxy (M51) looks like a fuzzy pinwheel.

Even a small telescope will give you an idea of the vastness of the Universe!

Even astronomers can't always believe their eyes!

Astronomers are human, too! About 100 years ago, one astronomer saw a small moon of Saturn that was never seen again. Perhaps it was a mistake or a flaw in the telescope. In 1937, an asteroid was spotted flying just 500,000 miles (800,000 km) from Earth. It has never been seen again. Sometimes, astronomers see small changes on the Moon, which is supposedly a dead world. Mistakes? Or is the Moon not quite dead? The sky is full of mysteries — even today!

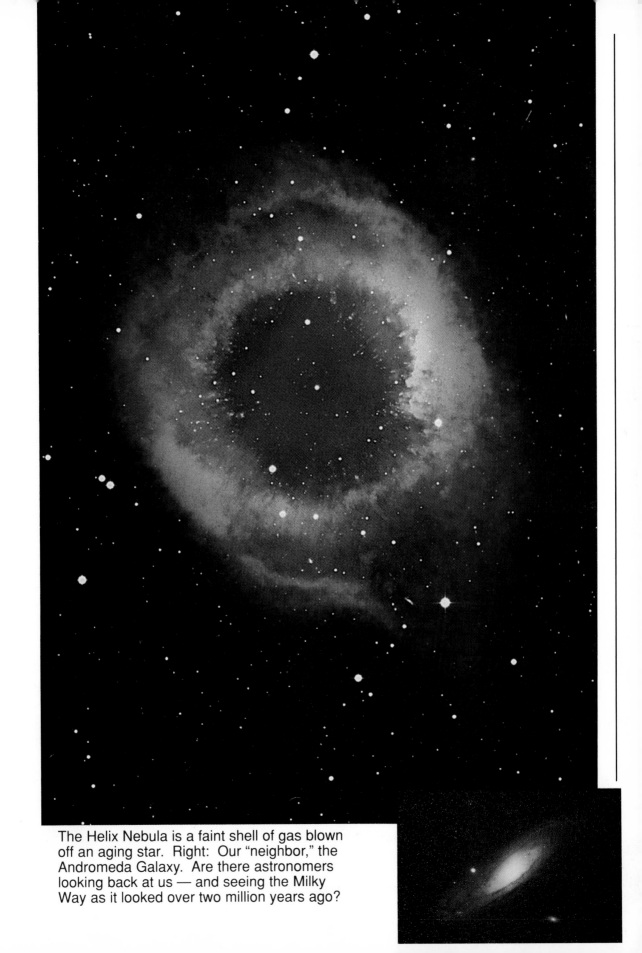

The Helix Nebula is a faint shell of gas blown off an aging star. Right: Our "neighbor," the Andromeda Galaxy. Are there astronomers looking back at us — and seeing the Milky Way as it looked over two million years ago?

Fact File: Constellations in the Southern Hemisphere

Many of the constellations that we in the Northern Hemisphere see are named after the gods and heroes of ancient Greek mythology, or after objects that were in common use even in ancient times.

But what about the stars that people in the Southern Hemisphere see? Not many people in the Northern Hemisphere thought or cared about the Southern Hemisphere sky until late in the 16th century, when explorers needed to map the southern sky so they could navigate their ships at night.

So when astronomers did give names to the constellations of the Southern Hemisphere, they did not use names from ancient myths. Instead, they named the constellations after animals found in explorers' travels and instruments used to find their way amid the sea and stars.

Here is a file of just a few of the many constellations you can spot in the skies of the Southern Hemisphere.

When humans travel to distant planets, stars, and galaxies in the future, the star patterns they see will be different from the constellations we know. What beings or things will they name their constellations after?

Here is a view of the Southern Hemisphere sky showing some of the constellations featured in the chart on the next page. Also shown are the Southern Cross, or Crux, which is a key constellation for finding one's way around the sky south of the equator; the Small Magellanic Cloud and the Large Magellanic Cloud, which are two "small" neighboring galaxies; the Coal Sack, a dark, dusty nebula; and a portion of our very own Galaxy, the Milky Way.

Name of Constellation	Description	Named by	Year
Dorado Tucana Apus	Goldfish Toucan Bird of Paradise	Johann Bayer (Germany)	1603
Circinus Horologium Antlia Telescopium	Compasses Clock Air Pump Telescope	Nicholas Louis Lacaille (France)	1750s

EAST   SOUTH   WEST

More Books About Astronomy

Here are more books that contain information about astronomy. If you are interested in them, check your library or bookstore.

Ancient Astronomy. Asimov (Gareth Stevens)
Astro-Dome Book: 3-D Map of the Night Sky. Hunig (Constellation)
Astronomy Basics. Litpak (Prentice-Hall)
Discovering the Stars. Santrey (Troll)
Far Out: How to Create Your Own Star World. West (Carolrhoda Books)
Find the Constellations. Rey (Houghton Mifflin)
Night Sky. Barrett (Franklin Watts)
Sun Dogs and Shooting Stars: A Skywatcher's Calendar. Branley (Houghton Mifflin)

Places to Visit

You can map the planets and stars without leaving Earth. Here are some museums, observatories, planetariums, and centers where you can stargaze to your heart's content.

MacDonald Observatory
Austin, Texas

Gordon MacMillan Southam Observatory
Vancouver, British Columbia

Hayden Planetarium — American Museum
New York, New York

Star Theatre — Edmonton Space Sciences Centre
Edmonton, Alberta

Dow Planetarium
Montreal, Quebec

Adler Planetarium
Chicago, Illinois

For More Information About Astronomy

Here are some people you can write to or call for more information about astronomy. Be sure to tell them exactly what you want to know about or see. Remember to include your age, full name, and address.

Astronomical "Hotline" for up-to-date descriptions of the sky:
Dial (416) 586-5751
The McLaughlin Planetarium
Toronto, Ontario

For monthly sky maps:
National Museum of Science and Technology
Astronomy Division
2380 Lancaster Road
Ottawa, Ontario K1A 0M8, Canada

For catalogs of slides, posters, and other astronomy materials:
AstroMedia Order Department
1027 N. 7th Street
Milwaukee, Wisconsin 53233

Sky Publishing Corporation
49 Bay State Road
Cambridge, Massachusetts 02238-1290

Selectory Sales
Astronomical Society of the Pacific
1290 24th Avenue
San Francisco, California 94122

Hansen Planetarium
15 South State Street
Salt Lake City, Utah 84111

Glossary

Andromeda Galaxy: a huge collection of stars in the constellation Andromeda that can be seen with a telescope.

axis: the imaginary line through the center of a planet around which the planet rotates. The axis of Earth extends from the North Pole to the South Pole.

billion: In this book, the number represented by 1 followed by nine zeroes — 1,000,000,000. In some places, such as the United Kingdom (Britain), this number is called "a thousand million." In these places, one billion would then be represented by 1 followed by *12* zeroes — 1,000,000,000,000: a million million, known as a trillion in North America.

constellation: a grouping of stars in the sky that seems to trace out a familiar pattern, figure, or symbol. Constellations are often named after that which they are thought to resemble.

filters: devices in telescopes that partially eliminate reflections and glare to protect the eyes from dangerous light.

galaxy: any of the many large groupings of stars, gas, and dust that exist in the Universe. Our Galaxy is known as the Milky Way.

moon: a natural satellite revolving around a planet.

"new Moon": that crescent-shaped bit of the lighted side of the Moon that we see as the Moon begins a new cycle.

Northern Hemisphere: the half of Earth north of the Equator.

observatory: a building or other structure designed for watching and recording celestial objects or events.

phases: the periods when Venus, Mercury, and our Moon are partly lit by the Sun. It takes about one month for Earth's Moon to progress from full Moon to full Moon.

"pointers": the two stars at the bowl end of the Big Dipper that point toward the North Star, or Polaris.

prehistoric: the period in history before writing was invented.

pulsar: a neutron star sending out rapid pulses of light or other radiation.

quasar: a "quasi-stellar," or "star-like," core of a galaxy that may have a large black hole at its center.

red giant: a huge star that develops when the hydrogen in an aging star runs low and the extra heat makes the star expand. The outer layers then change to a cool red.

reflector: a type of telescope that uses curved mirrors to concentrate light.

refractor: a type of telescope that uses lenses to concentrate light.

revolve: to go around completely or circle, as Earth revolves around the Sun.

Stonehenge: a place in southwestern England that may have been an ancient observatory.

summer solstice: in the Northern Hemisphere, the time of year, around June 22, when the Sun is highest in the sky. The summer solstice marks the official start of summer. The winter solstice, when the Sun is lowest in the sky, is around December 22. This marks the start of winter.

Universe: all existing things, including Earth and the Sun, Solar system, galaxies, and all that which is or may be beyond.

variable star: a star whose light grows brighter, then dimmer.

zodiac: the band of 12 constellations across the sky that represents the paths of the Sun, the Moon, Mercury, Venus, Mars, Jupiter, and Saturn.

Index

Aldebaran 16-17
Alpha Centauri 23
Altair 12-13
Andromeda (Chained Maiden) 14-15
Andromeda Galaxy 14-15, 26-27
Antares 12-13
Aquarius (Water Carrier) 19
Aquila (Eagle) 12-13
Arcturus 10-11
Aries (Ram) 19

Betelgeuse 16-17, 25
Big Dipper, the 8-9, 10-11
Boötes (Herdsman) 10-11

Cancer (Crab) 19
Canis Major (Great Dog) 16-17
Capricorn (Goat) 19
Cassiopeia (Queen) 8-9
Cetus (Whale) 14-15
Coal Sack (nebula) 28-29
Crux (Southern Cross) 8, 28-29
Cygnus (Swan) 12-13

Deneb 12-13

Earth 5, 6-7, 16, 18-19, 23, 25, 26
Egypt, ancient 11, 16
England, ancient 6
Evening Star (Venus) 21

Gemini (Twins) 19
Greeks, ancient 28

Helix Nebula 27
Hercules 26

Jupiter 18, 22-23

Large Magellanic Cloud 28-29
Leo (Lion) 10-11, 19
Libra (Scales) 19
Lunar eclipse 6
Lyra (Lyre) 12-13

Mars 18, 23
Mercury 18, 20-21
Milky Way Galaxy 12-13, 23, 26-27, 28-29
Mira 14-15
Moon 4, 6-7, 10-11, 18, 20, 22, 24, 26
Morning Star (Venus) 21

Neptune 23
Neutron stars 25
North Pole, Earth's 5
North Star 5, 11

Observatories 6
Orion (Hunter) 16-17
Orion Nebula 16-17

Pegasus (Flying Horse) 14-15
Phases 6-7, 20-21, 23
Pisces (Fish) 19
Pluto 23
"Pointers" 9
Polaris (North Star) 5, 8-9, 11, 12

Red giant stars 12
Regulus 10-11
Rigel 16-17

Sagittarius (Archer) 12-13, 19
Saturn 18, 22, 26
Scorpius (Scorpion) 12-13, 19
Sirius 16-17
Small Magellanic Cloud 28-29
Solar system 23
South Pole, Earth's 8
Southern Cross 8, 28-29
Spica 10-11
Square of Pegasus 14-15
Stonehenge 6
Summer solstice 6
Sun 4-5, 6, 10-11, 12, 16, 18-19, 21, 23, 25

Taurus (Bull) 16-17, 19
Telescopes 12, 14, 22-23, 24-25, 26

Universe 26
Uranus 23
Ursa Major (Great Bear) 8-9, 10-11

Variable stars 14
Vega 12-13
Venus 18, 20-21, 22
Virgo (Maiden) 10-11, 19

Whirlpool Galaxy 26
White dwarf stars 25

zodiac, constellations of the 10-11, 18-19
Zodiac of Dendera 11

The publishers wish to thank the following for permission to reproduce copyright material: front cover, pp. 7 (lower), 20, 22 (upper), © Frank Zullo; p. 4, © Anglo-Australian Telescope Board, David Malin, 1980; pp. 6-7, Lick Observatory Photographs; pp. 8, 9, 10, 11 (upper), 12, 13 (upper), 14, 15 (upper), 16, 17, © Julian Baum, 1988; p. 11 (lower), photograph courtesy of Julian Baum; p. 13 (lower), Science Photo Library; p. 15 (lower), National Optical Astronomy Observatories; pp. 17 (lower), 21 (lower), 23 (both), 26, courtesy of NASA; pp. 18-19, © Brad Greenwood, courtesy of Hansen Planetarium; pp. 19 (lower), 24 (upper), 25 (lower), © Matthew Groshek; p. 21 upper, Jet Propulsion Laboratory; p. 22 (lower), © California Institute of Technology, 1965; pp. 24 (lower), 25 (upper), Meade Instruments; p. 27 (upper), © Anglo-Australian Telescope Board, David Malin, 1979; p. 27 (lower), © California Institute of Technology, 1959; p. 28, © Julian Baum and Matthew Groshek, 1988.

520
ASI

cop.1

Asimov, Isaac
    The space spotter's
    guide

ST. GABRIEL SCHOOL